# France

by Adam Markovics

Consultant: Marjorie Faulstich Orellana, PhD
Professor of Urban Schooling
University of California, Los Angeles

BEARPORT
PUBLISHING

New York, New York

## Credits

Cover, © StevanZZ/Shutterstock and © Rob Marmion/Shutterstock; TOC, © Ian 2010/Shutterstock; 4, © Ventdusud/iStock; 5T, © Alena Vezza/Shutterstock; 5B, © Branislav Nenin/Shutterstock; 7, © muratart/Shutterstock; 8, © Venturelli Luca/Shutterstock; 9, © LiliGraphie/Shutterstock; 10, © Gayane/Shutterstock; 11 (T to B), © Igor Lateci/Shutterstock, © Eric Isselee/Shutterstock, and © ecobo/iStock; 12L, © Bridgeman Images; 12–13, © Mario Fourmy/laif/Redux; 14, © Everett–Art/Shutterstock; 15, © Musee de la Ville de Paris, Musee du Petit–Palais, France/Bridgeman Images; 16–17, © Augustin Lazaroiu/iStock; 17R, © majeczka/Shutterstock; 18T, © Goddard_Photography/iStock; 18B, © Ekaterina Pokrovsky/Shutterstock; 19, © Baloncici/Shutterstock; 20, © Sam Bloomberg–Rissman/AGE Fotostock; 21, © Rido/Shutterstock; 22T, © cristi180884/Shutterstock; 22B, © andreasnikolas/Shutterstock; 23, © Rrrainbow/iStock; 24–25, © Radu Razvan/Shutterstock; 25R, © Vikulin/Shutterstock; 26, © posztos/Shutterstock; 27, Public Domain; 28L, © Ditty_about_summer/Shutterstock; 28–29, © TPX/Prisma/AGE Fotostock; 30T, © Tony Kunz/Shutterstock and © spinetta/Shutterstock; 30B, © Ruslan Mitin/Shutterstock; 31 (T to B), Public Domain, © Kiev.Victor/Shutterstock, © TomasSereda/iStock, © Everett–Art/Shutterstock, © Phillip Minnis/Shutterstock, and © Production Perig/Shutterstock; 32, © tristan tan/Shutterstock.

Publisher: Kenn Goin
Senior Editor: Joyce Tavolacci
Creative Director: Spencer Brinker
Design: Debrah Kaiser
Photo Researcher: Thomas Persano

*Library of Congress Cataloging-in-Publication Data*

Names: Markovics, Adam, author.
Title: France / by Adam Markovics.
Description: New York, New York : Bearport Publishing, [2018] | Series:
  Countries we come from | Includes bibliographical references and index. |
  Audience: Ages 5–8.
Identifiers: LCCN 2017014714 (print) | LCCN 2017015088 (ebook) |
ISBN 9781684023110 (ebook) | ISBN 9781684022571 (library)
Subjects: LCSH: France—Juvenile literature.
Classification: LCC DC17 (ebook) | LCC DC17 .M32 2018 (print) | DDC 944—dc23
LC record available at https://lccn.loc.gov/2017014714

For more information, write to Bearport Publishing Company, Inc., 45 West 21st Street, Suite 3B, New York, New York 10010. Printed in the United States of America.

10 9 8 7 6 5 4 3 2 1

# Contents

STUNNING

Stylish

Friendly

Welcome to France—one of the largest countries in Europe!

More than 64 million people live there.

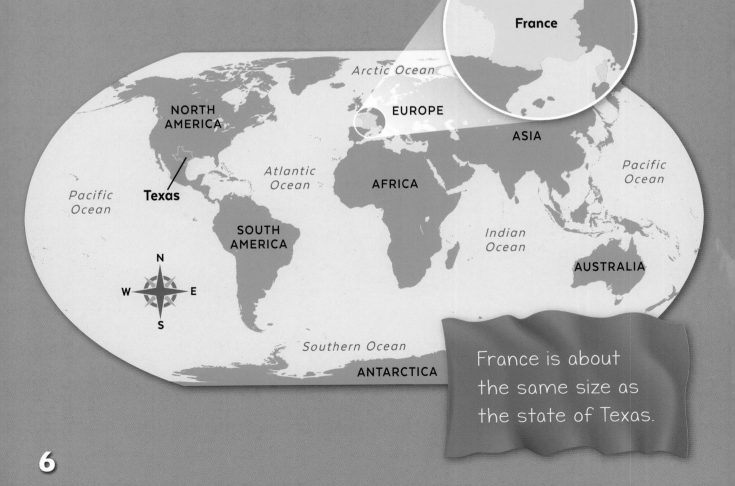

France

Arctic Ocean

NORTH AMERICA

EUROPE

ASIA

Pacific Ocean

Atlantic Ocean

Texas

AFRICA

Pacific Ocean

SOUTH AMERICA

Indian Ocean

AUSTRALIA

N
W    E
S

Southern Ocean

ANTARCTICA

France is about the same size as the state of Texas.

Sacré-Coeur church in Paris

7

France has towering mountains.
Europe's tallest mountain, Mont Blanc, is located there.

It rises more than 15,700 feet (4,785 m)!

Along the southeast coast of France are beautiful beaches.

There is rich farmland throughout France.

Many farmers grow grapes to make wine.

Some of the grapes
are used to make
a bubbly wine.

It's called champagne
(sham-PEYN).

champagne

Farmers also raise
cows, sheep, and goats.
Their milk is used to
make 400 kinds of
French cheese!

Early humans first lived in France about 1.6 million years ago.

In southwest France, there are **ancient** paintings inside caves.

The paintings are around 20,000 years old!

The cave paintings show horses and other animals.

visitors inside a model of one of the ancient caves

For most of its history, kings ruled France.

In 1789, the people of France took back power during the French Revolution.

Afterward, France became a free country.

Napoleon Bonaparte was a famous **military** leader. He ruled France from 1799 to 1815.

15

The **capital** of France is Paris.

It's also the country's largest city.

More than two million people live there.

The Eiffel Tower soars above Paris. It's one of France's most famous **landmarks**.

People like to wander Paris's winding streets.

They may stop to sip coffee at one of the city's many outdoor cafés.

Then they might grab a crusty baguette (ba-GET) at a local bakery.

Paris has some of the best bakeries in the world.

The main language in France is French.

This is how you say *please*:

**S'il vous plaît**
(SEE VOO PLEH)

# This is how you say *good night*:
## **Bonne nuit** (BOHN NWEE)

More than 75 million people speak French worldwide.

French food is famous around the world.

People enjoy golden, flaky croissants (kwah-SAHNTS).

Macarons (mah–kuh–ROHNS) are French almond cookies. They come in a rainbow of colors.

Thin pancakes called crepes (KREYPS) are cooked on a hot griddle.

# Which sports are popular in France?

Crowds line the streets to watch Le Tour de France.

It's the most famous bicycle race in the world!

French fans also enjoy soccer and basketball.

There are hundreds of art museums in France.

The biggest is the Louvre (LOOV-ruh) in Paris.

The Louvre used to be a royal **palace**.

It holds the famous Mona Lisa painting.

the Mona Lisa

Is she smiling— or not?

France is the most visited country in the world!

Around 80 million **tourists** visit the country each year.

The Palace of Versailles is a popular place to visit. It was the home of King Louis XIV.

# Fast Facts

**Capital city**: Paris

**Population of France**: More than 64 million

**Main language**: French

**Money**: Euro

**Major religions**: Christian, Muslim, and Jewish

**Neighboring countries include**: Belgium, Germany, Italy, Luxembourg, Monaco, Spain, and Switzerland

**Cool Fact:** The average French person eats 500 snails each year!

**ancient** (AYN-shunt)  very old

**capital** (KAP-uh-tuhl)  a city where a country's government is based

**landmarks** (LAND-mahrks)  objects or features of a place that are easily recognized

**military** (MIL-uh-*ter*-ee)  having to do with armies or war

**palace** (PAL-iss)  the grand home of a king, queen, or other ruler

**tourists** (TOOR-ists)  people who travel and visit places for pleasure

**31**

# Index

## Read More

**Colson, Mary.** *France (Countries Around the World).* Portsmouth, NH: Heinemann (2011).

**Grack, Rachel.** *France (Blastoff! Readers: Exploring Countries).* Minnetonka, MN: Bellwether (2010).

## Learn More Online

To learn more about France, visit
**www.bearportpublishing.com/CountriesWeComeFrom**

## About the Author

Adam Markovics lives in Ossining, New York. On a trip to Paris, he once spent a small fortune shipping the most delicious French macarons he had ever tasted back to his family in the United States.